Pretending Poems

Compiled by John Foster

Contents

Acknowledgements

The Editor and Publisher wish to thank the following who have kindly given permission for the use of copyright material:

John Foster for 'Close your eyes', 'My special friend' and 'Pretending' all © 1991 John Foster; Trevor Harvey for 'Sometimes I pretend' © 1991 Trevor Harvey; Charles Thomson for 'Pirates' © 1991 Charles Thomson; Irene Yates for 'Adventure at breakfast time' © 1991 Irene Yates.

Sometimes I pretend

Sometimes I pretend
I am a giant,
With feet so HUGE
I squash the houses
In our street
Each time I move!

Sometimes I pretend
I am an ant,
With feet so small
I tiptoe by
And no one knows
I'm there at all!

Trevor Harvey

Close your eyes

Close your eyes. Count to ten.
When you open them again
I will be a DRAGON
With scales like silver coins.

Close your eyes. Count to ten.
When you open them again
I will be a ROBOT
With eyes like bright red traffic lights.

John Foster

Adventure at breakfast time

Here comes Batman
Zooming across our garden
To save the cat from
The dinosaur
That lives next door.

And here comes She-ra
Zapping along the front path
To check the milk bottles
For bat-juice, dragonfly-wings
And other
Very nasty things.

And here comes Egon
Zooming through the kitchen door
To rescue the dog from
The ghost
That slurps the butter
Off my toast.

And here comes our Dad
Zapping down the stairs
To give them all a
Telling off
And send them away
Because
I can't go out to play
Till I've finished
My breakfast.

Irene Yates

Pirates

Let's play pirates.
Let's pretend.
This chair's a ship:
the front's my end.

Yes, great!

I'm the captain.
You're the crew,
so I can tell you
what to do.

Yes, great!

OK then, you're
a lower rank,
so now you've got
to walk the plank.

Yes, grea

a

a

a

r

g

h

h

h

!

Charles Thomson

Pretending

I sit on the swing and I fly up high.
I am a brave spaceman
   exploring the sky.

I stand on my bed and I jump
  up and down.
I tumble and fall. I'm a circus clown.

I sit in my bath and I play with my ship.
There are rocks and sharks.
It's a dangerous trip.

I lie in my bed and I close my eyes tight.
My bed is a ship which I sail
    through the night.

John Foster

My special friend

At night when it's dark
I like to pretend
My bed is being guarded
By my special friend.

I like to pretend
As I snuggle down tight
That my friend will guard me
As I sleep through the night.

John Foster